ECONOMIC ISSUES 17

Liberalizing Capital Movements

Some Analytical Issues

Barry Eichengreen
Michael Mussa
Giovanni Dell'Ariccia
Enrica Detragiache
Gian Maria Milesi-Ferretti
Andrew Tweedie

INTERNATIONAL MONETARY FUND
WASHINGTON, D.C.

Series Editor
J.R. Morrison
IMF External Relations Department

Cover design and composition
Massoud Etemadi, Julio R. Prego, and
the IMF Graphics Section

ISBN 1-55775-792-5
ISSN 1020-5098

Published February 1999

To order IMF publications, please contact:

International Monetary Fund, Publication Services
700 19th Street, N.W., Washington, D.C. 20431, U.S.A.
Tel: (202) 623-7430 Telefax: (202) 623-7201
E-mail: publications@imf.org
Internet: http://www.imf.org

Preface

The Economic Issues series aims to make available to a broad readership of nonspecialists some of the economic research being produced on topical issues by IMF staff. The series draws mainly from IMF Working Papers, which are technical papers produced by IMF staff members and visiting scholars, as well as from policy-related research papers.

This Economic Issue draws on material originally contained in IMF Occasional Paper 172, *Capital Account Liberalization: Theoretical and Practical Aspects,* by a staff team led by Barry Eichengreen and Michael Mussa, with Giovanni Dell'Ariccia, Enrica Detragiache, Gian Maria Milesi-Ferretti, and Andrew Tweedie. This version was prepared by Pamela Bradley of the External Relations Department. Readers may purchase the Occasional Paper ($18; $15 to full-time faculty members and students at universities and colleges) from IMF Publication Services.

Liberalizing Capital Movements: Some Analytical Issues

The explosive growth of international financial transactions and capital flows is one of the most far-reaching economic developments of the late twentieth century. Net private capital flows to developing countries tripled—to more than $150 billion a year during 1995–97 from roughly $50 billion a year during 1987–89. At the same time, the ratio of private capital flows to domestic investment in developing countries increased to 20 percent in 1996 from only 3 percent in 1990.

Powerful forces have driven the rapid growth of international capital flows, including the trend in both industrial and developing countries toward economic liberalization and the globalization of trade. Revolutionary changes in information and communications technologies have transformed the financial services industry worldwide. Computer links enable investors to access information on asset prices at minimal cost on a real-time basis, while increased computing power enables them to rapidly calculate correlations among asset prices and between asset prices and other variables. At the same time, new technologies make it increasingly difficult for governments to control either inward or outward international capital flows when they wish to do so.

All this means that the liberalization of capital markets—and, with it, likely increases in the volume and the volatility of international capital flows—is an ongoing and, to some extent, irreversible process. It has contributed to higher investment, faster growth, and rising living standards in many countries. But financial liberalization—both domestic and international—has also been associated with costly financial crises in several cases. This underscores that liberalization carries risks as well as benefits and has major implications for the policies that governments will find it feasible and desirable to follow.

This paper addresses the potential gains and risks of open capital markets by first looking at what classical economic theory suggests about the benefits of capital mobility and then examining the counterarguments arising from problems of incomplete information and other distortions. It shows that the risks of removing controls on flows of capital across national borders are similar to those associated with removing controls on domestic financial institutions. The paper then explores how to manage liberalization to minimize the risks and maximize the benefits.

What Theory Says

The Classic Case for Capital Mobility

The flows of capital—debt, portfolio equity, and direct and real estate investment—between one country and others are recorded in the capital account of its balance of payments. Outflows include residents' purchases of foreign assets and repayment of foreign loans; inflows include foreigners' investments in home-country financial markets and property and loans to home-country residents. Freeing transactions like these from restrictions—that is, allowing capital to flow freely in or out of a country without controls or restrictions—is known as capital account liberalization.

Classic economic theory argues that international capital mobility allows countries with limited savings to attract financing for productive domestic investment projects, that it enables investors to diversify their portfolios, that it spreads investment risk more broadly, and that it promotes intertemporal trade—the trading of goods today for goods in the future. More specifically:

- Capital mobility means that households, firms, or even countries can smooth consumption by borrowing money from abroad when incomes are low in the home country and repaying when incomes are high. The ability to borrow abroad can thus dampen business cycles by allowing households and firms to continue buying and investing when domestic production and incomes have fallen.
- By lending money abroad, households and firms can reduce their vulnerability to domestic economic disturbances. Companies can protect themselves against sudden cost increases in the home country, for example, by investing in branch plants in several countries. Capital mobility thus enables investors to achieve higher risk-adjusted rates of return. In turn, higher rates of return can encourage saving and investment that deliver faster economic growth.

Information Problems and Their Implications

At the theoretical level, the controversy over the benefits of financial liberalization reflects diverging views on whether free capital movements can deliver an efficient allocation of resources. Critics of the "efficient markets" view argue that liberalized financial markets are so distorted by incomplete information and other problems that transactions often yield outcomes harmful to the general welfare. They point out that information in financial markets is pervasively "asymmetric"—that is, one party to the financial transaction (such as a loan officer) has less information about it than the other party (perhaps a borrower with a high tolerance for risk-taking). Such information gaps give rise to several problems—known in the academic literature as adverse selection, moral hazard, and herding (see Box)—that plague financial markets in particular. At a minimum,

Lemons, Herds, and Other Problems of Asymmetric Information

Information is "asymmetric" when one party to an economic relationship or transaction has less information about it than the other party or parties. While asymmetric information characterizes many markets (such as that for used cars, where sellers know which cars are "lemons"), some economists believe it particularly pervades financial markets. Three problems in particular—called adverse selection, moral hazard, and herding behavior—have been associated with asymmetric information. Each has the potential to lead to inefficient and unstable financial markets.

Adverse selection. In financial markets, lenders frequently have incomplete knowledge of the creditworthiness—or quality—of borrowers. Given that lenders cannot fully evaluate the creditworthiness of each borrower, they will be willing to pay a price for a security (that is, lend money at an interest rate) that reflects only the *average* quality of firms (or borrowers) issuing securities. That price is likely to be less than the fair market value for high-quality firms but more than fair market value for low-quality firms. Because the managers of high-quality firms know that their securities are undervalued (or, their borrowing costs are excessive), they will avoid borrowing on the market. Only low-quality firms will wish to sell securities. Since high-quality firms will issue few securities, many projects that would have generated profits will not be undertaken. At the same time, the less successful or even loss-making projects of low-quality firms will be financed—an inefficient outcome.

Moral hazard. This occurs when one party to a transaction has both the incentive and the ability to shift costs onto the other party. For example, homeowners with fire insurance may be less careful than the uninsured about smoking in their homes, knowing the cost

they say, such asymmetries can lead to inefficiencies; in the extreme, they can lead to costly financial crises.

A chief concern here is moral hazard—the risk that investors will expect governments to bail them out—created by government guarantees for financial institutions in the absence of adequate safeguards or sufficient incentives for market discipline to police excessive risk-taking. Important, too, are concerns about herding of their carelessness is shifted to the fire department, the insurance company, and, indirectly, other purchasers of fire insurance. In financial markets, when information is asymmetric, a creditor may not be able to observe whether a borrower will invest in a risky project or a safe project, and, if the borrower is protected by limited liability or guarantees of some sort, too much investment in risky projects will result.

An extreme case of moral hazard occurs when companies or banks with negative net worth borrow to ***gamble for redemption***—that is, invest in ventures with a high potential payoff (and thus potential rescue from bankruptcy) but a low probability of success. Over time, lenders will become more reluctant to make loans, and the quantity of money being invested will be less than the amount that makes sense from an economic standpoint.

Herding behavior. Lenders may try to follow the lead of someone they believe to be better informed about, say, the probability a certain bank will fail. Herding behavior can also occur when investors lack information about the quality of those who manage their funds. Low-quality money managers will find it rational to emulate the investment decisions of other managers in order not to be found out. And herding can make sense when the payoff to an agent adopting an action increases because many other agents adopt the same action. For example, individual currency traders may be too small to exhaust a central bank's reserves and force a currency devaluation, but simultaneous sales by several traders can bring about such a devaluation, thus rewarding the first agent's decision to sell the currency. It is easy to see that in the presence of asymmetric or incomplete information, investors will quite rationally take actions that can amplify price movements and precipitate sudden crises.

behavior that can lead to sharp investor reactions, unpredictable market movements, and even financial crises.

Is, then, the theoretical presumption that market liberalization enhances the efficiency of resource allocation correct? A more accurate statement is that international financial liberalization, like domestic liberalization, unambiguously improves efficiency only when accompanied by policies to *limit* moral hazard, adverse selection, herding behavior, and related problems, and to *contain* their potentially damaging consequences. As discussed later, these policies include prudential supervision and regulation combined with careful design of a lender-of-last-resort facility to limit the scope for financial market participants to take on too much risk and to contain potentially systemic disturbances. In addition, every effort must be made to encourage world-class standards for accounting, auditing, and information disclosure, which facilitate sound rules of corporate governance and protect investors and lenders from fraud and unfair practices.

Capital Account Liberalization and Crises

Economic theory aside, experience has demonstrated that liberalizing the capital account before the home-country financial system has been strengthened can contribute to serious economic problems. In particular, domestic and international financial liberalization heighten the risk of crises if not supported by robust prudential supervision and regulation (and appropriate macroeconomic policies). Domestic liberalization, by intensifying competition in the financial sector, removes a cushion protecting intermediaries from the consequences of bad loan and management practices. It can allow home banks to expand risky activities at rates that far exceed their capacity to manage them and permit home banks with negative net worth to use expensive funding to "gamble for redemption" (see Box). By granting home banks access to complex derivative financial instruments, it can make evaluating bank balance sheets more difficult and stretch the capacity of regulators to monitor risks.

External financial liberalization can magnify the effects of inadequate policies. By allowing the entry of foreign banks, external liberalization, like its domestic counterpart, can squeeze margins and remove home banks' cushion against loan losses. Like domestic financial liberalization, it can facilitate gambling for redemption, in this case by offering access to an abundant supply of offshore funding and risky foreign investments. A currency crisis or unexpected devaluation can undermine the solvency of banks and bank customers who, under lax regulation, have built up large liabilities denominated in foreign currency and are unprotected against foreign exchange rate changes. Moreover, capital account liberalization, which increases the potential for sudden reversals of capital inflows, can force the national authorities to hike interest rates even more dramatically to defend a currency peg under attack, something they may be loath to do when the banking system is already fragile. Thus, external financial liberalization increases the scope for lack of confidence in the banking system and in the currency peg to feed on one another in a vicious spiral.

Recognizing these possibilities, the IMF's policy-setting committee—the Interim Committee—and subsequently the finance ministers and central bank governors of the Group of Seven industrial nations, in the fall of 1998, stressed that a country opening its capital account must do so in an orderly, gradual, and well-sequenced manner.

These are ongoing issues, but two points about these dangers require emphasis:

The mechanisms through which internal and external financial liberalization can expose threats to financial stability are largely the same.

As an inevitable—and desirable—consequence of improving financial and economic efficiency, both internal and external liberalization tend to squeeze margins and leave less leeway for poor loan and management practices. Both give banks and other intermediaries opportunities to profit by carefully assessing and prudently managing risky investments. But both also widen the opening for imprudent or improper exploitation of those expanded opportunities. There is nothing unique or different about external financial liberalization in this regard.

It is not financial liberalization that is at the root of the problem but rather weak management in the financial sector and inadequate prudential supervision and regulation, whose consequences are magnified by liberalization.

Systemic Policy Issues

In an ideal world, those who invest would bear the risk associated with that investment. Banks and other financial market participants would be prudent in their investment choices and forced by their shareholders and clients to adopt best-practice accounting, auditing, and disclosure standards. In the real world, where techniques of risk management are not always well developed, auditing and accounting practices leave much to be desired, and other distortions interfere with banks' ability to manage risk, prudential regulation has an especially important role.

Prudential regulation seeks to (1) reinforce private incentives for banks (and other participants in financial markets) to recognize the risks they are taking, and (2) enable the authorities to monitor potential threats to systemic stability so they can take corrective measures if needed. Prudential regulation falls short when it allows financial institutions to expand risky activities faster than their capacity to manage them, allows banks and bank customers to build up dangerous unhedged exposures, or allows distressed banks to gamble for redemption. (In some cases, measures to address financial and organizational restructuring of major banks may also be needed to remove the incentive to gamble for redemption.) Appropriate prudential regulation, by contrast, encourages banks to put aside reserves that many be needed when events suddenly interrupt their access to foreign funding (including external events such as a change in world interest rates, for example, or a crisis in a neighboring country).

A century or more of historical experience points to the need, in most countries, for central banks to provide lender-of-last-resort services to prevent illiquid financial markets from seizing up in periods of general distress. This backstopping function, though essential, is also a source of some moral hazard. The appropriate response for national authorities is rigorous prudential supervision and regulation combined with careful design of the lender-of-last-resort facility.

At the international level, policymakers must also address what should be done on the side of the suppliers of capital flows. Recent efforts to improve data on flows of international credit from (and through) major capital markets to emerging market countries should help alert both lenders and borrowers to excessive concentrations of debt, especially short-term debt. In addition, if banks were more accurate in assessing the riskiness of their interbank lending, in particular their loans in emerging markets, they might be more conservative in setting limits to such lending, thus reducing the potential contagion effects of a financial crisis in one of those countries.

Research and experience confirm that sound macroeconomic policies are also key to successful liberalization. They help prevent the buildup of destabilizing imbalances in financial markets, as well as offset the damaging effects of financial crises as the herd stampedes to the downside. Prudent fiscal policy that prevents the ballooning of large deficits will avoid the temptation to rely on foreign loans that might create debt-management problems, reduce creditworthiness, or weaken an economy's ability to manage external shocks. Monetary policy can be used to counteract disorderly markets (e.g., by raising interest rates temporarily, capital flight can be reversed), and fiscal and monetary policy can be used to ameliorate economic contraction in a downturn (monetary and fiscal expansion can raise output and employment and can be used to counteract the effects of temporary disturbances).

Sequencing Matters

The sequencing of capital account liberalization is an important but complicated issue. Countries vary greatly: in their levels of economic and financial development, in their institutional structures, in their legal systems and business practices, and in their capacity to manage change in a host of areas relevant for financial liberalization. Accordingly, there is no cookbook recipe for the sequence of steps to follow and no general guideline for how long the process should take.

Presumably, a country with a fully liberalized domestic financial system that had firmly put in place the safeguards necessary to ensure its successful operation could proceed almost immediately and with confidence to full capital account liberalization. This advice, however, generally applies to countries (mainly the industrial countries) that already have quite liberal policies toward international capital.

Alternatively, maintaining tight restrictions on virtually all forms of international financial flows until the domestic financial system is fully and successfully liberalized is generally not advisable. International and domestic liberalization can reinforce one another and can benefit from parallel development. In countries where entrenched interests and policy inertia inhibit reform, external pressures created by the opening of capital markets can provide the needed impetus.

Where domestic preparations are well advanced, essentially full international liberalization should be able to proceed relatively rapidly, perhaps within a decade or so for the more advanced emerging markets. Where the essential infrastructure for a liberal and stable financial system is not well developed, full liberalization, both domestic and international, will generally require more time.

On sequencing, a few general principles are worth noting:

- Although direct foreign investment sometimes raises concerns about foreign ownership and control, such investment can bring considerable benefits, including technology transfers and more efficient business practices. Also, because foreign direct investment flows are less prone to sudden reversals in a panic than bank loans and debt financing, they do not generate the same acute problems of financial crises as do sharp reversals of debt flows. Thus, liberalizing inward direct investment should generally be an attractive component of a broader program of liberalization.
- It is usually a mistake to liberalize the domestic banking system or to open it fully to inflows if important parts of the system are insolvent or likely to be pushed into insolvency by liberalization. As a general rule, nonviable institutions should be weeded out and remaining banks put on a sound footing before liberalizing or opening the domestic banking system.
- Because banking systems play a central role in the financial affairs of most emerging market countries, capital flows to and through the domestic banking system are already significantly liberalized in many of these countries. Reversing this situation by going back to detailed restrictions on capital flows through domestic banks hardly seems sensible. But the fact that capital inflows are already a reality only highlights the danger of removing most restrictions on capital account transactions too quickly, before major problems in the domestic financial system have been addressed. Inadequate accounting, auditing, and disclosure practices weaken market discipline; implicit government guarantees encourage excessive, unsustainable capital inflows; and inadequate prudential supervision and regulation of domestic financial institutions and markets can breed

corruption, connected lending, and gambling for redemption. Countries in which these problems are severe should liberalize the capital account gradually, in conjunction with steps to eliminate these distortions.

- The domestic markets and financial infrastructure for portfolio investments in equities and debt instruments are not well developed in many emerging market countries. Creating the domestic infrastructure is necessary before these markets can be opened internationally. The economy can also benefit from the development of domestic financial markets that allow financial flows to be less heavily dependent on the banking system.
- Given the particular problems associated with short-term foreign debt, there may also be a case for liberalizing longer-term flows, particularly foreign direct investment, ahead of short-term capital inflows.
- Much of the above discussion has focused on the liberalization of capital inflows. Regarding the liberalization of capital outflows, the main concern arises when the restrictions to be removed are supporting either a significant macroeconomic imbalance or a distorted financial system. If an overvalued exchange rate has been maintained with the help of restrictions on capital outflows, then the government must be prepared to adjust the exchange rate when the restrictions are removed. Similarly, if policies have kept interest rates for savers artificially low, market participants must be prepared for a rise in rates. To avoid such costly accidents, countries should liberalize outflows after they have reduced macroeconomic imbalances and financial distortions to manageable proportions.

Summary and Conclusions

Financial liberalization is inevitable for countries that wish to take advantage of the substantial benefits—higher investment, faster growth, and rising living standards—of participating in the open world economic system in today's age of modern information and communications technologies. As recent events in Asia, in Russia, and in Latin America have again demonstrated, however, financial liberalization also has its dangers.

The classic case in favor of open, or liberalized, capital markets includes the more efficient allocation of savings, increased possibilities for diversification of investment risk, faster growth, and the dampening of business cycles. Critics of open capital markets, on the other hand, point to the inefficiencies resulting from adverse selection, moral hazard, and herding behavior, all of which are byproducts of asymmetric information—a situation in which not all parties to a transaction have equal information. Government policies, however, can lessen or mitigate the potential damage from asymmetric information problems.

If domestic financial markets are being distorted by inappropriate tax policy, shortcomings in bank supervision and regulation, or government guarantees of private sector liabilities, the solution is to properly sequence and supplement capital account liberalization by removing the distortion at the same time, or before, the capital account is liberalized. But to the extent that the problem lies in information asymmetries intrinsic to financial markets that cannot realistically be eliminated and give rise to systemic risks, there may be an argument for instituting policies to influence the volume of certain types of financial transactions.

For example, governments might wish to intervene to inhibit or counteract the excesses of herd behavior. Likewise, governments may wish to introduce taxes and policies that have tax-like effects (e.g., differential capital requirements or non-interest-earning deposit requirements) to discourage a particular category of capital account transaction, such as excessive dependence on short-term foreign debt. The use of such instruments, which modify behavior by altering relative prices, is not incompatible with the ultimate goal of capital account liberalization.

Has capital account liberalization been responsible for an increase in costly financial crises? Liberalizing the capital account before strengthening the domestic financial system certainly creates an environment conducive to serious economic problems and, potentially, financial crises. At the same time, reducing the barriers to the movement of savings has been a boon to economic development worldwide. And powerful and irreversible changes in information and communication technology have made highly mobile capital a fact of life. The solution to reconciling these considerations is not to revert to restrictions on capital flows, but to liberalize controls in an orderly, well-sequenced way, accompanied by sound macroeconomic policies, strengthened domestic financial systems, and improved transparency through disclosure of timely financial and economic information. With these safeguards, liberalization becomes not only inevitable but clearly beneficial.

The Economic Issues Series

1. *Growth in East Asia: What We Can and What We Cannot Infer.* Michael Sarel. 1996.
2. *Does the Exchange Rate Regime Matter for Inflation and Growth?* Atish R. Ghosh, Anne-Marie Gulde, Jonathan D. Ostry, and Holger Wolf. 1996.
3. *Confronting Budget Deficits.* 1996.
4. *Fiscal Reforms That Work.* C. John McDermott and Robert F. Wescott. 1996.
5. *Transformations to Open Market Operations: Developing Economies and Emerging Markets.* Stephen H. Axilrod. 1996.
6. *Why Worry About Corruption?* Paolo Mauro. 1997.
7. *Sterilizing Capital Inflows.* Jang-Yung Lee. 1997.
8. *Why Is China Growing So Fast?* Zuliu Hu and Mohsin S. Khan. 1997.
9. *Protecting Bank Deposits.* Gillian G. Garcia. 1997.
10. *Deindustrialization—Its Causes and Implications.* Robert Rowthorn and Ramana Ramaswamy. 1997.
11. *Does Globalization Lower Wages and Export Jobs?* Matthew J. Slaughter and Phillip Swagel. 1997.
12. *Roads to Nowhere: How Corruption in Public Investment Hurts Growth.* Vito Tanzi and Hamid Davoodi. 1998.
13. *Fixed or Flexible? Getting the Exchange Rate Right in the 1990s.* Francesco Caramazza and Jahangir Aziz. 1998.
14. *Lessons from Systemic Bank Restructuring.* Claudia Dziobek and Ceyla Pazarbaşıoğlu. 1998.
15. *Inflation Targeting as a Framework for Monetary Policy.* Guy Debelle, Paul Masson, Miguel Savastano, and Sunil Sharma. 1998.

16. *Should Equity Be a Goal of Economic Policy?* IMF Fiscal Affairs Department. 1998.

17. *Liberalizing Capital Movements: Some Analytical Issues.* Barry Eichengreen, Michael Mussa, Giovanni Dell'Ariccia, Enrica Detragiache, Gian Maria Milesi-Ferretti, and Andrew Tweedie. 1999.